DEER POOP OR BEAR POOP?

By George Fittleworth

Gareth Stevens
PUBLISHING

Please visit our website, www.garethstevens.com. For a free color catalog of all our high-quality books, call toll free 1-800-542-2595 or fax 1-877-542-2596.

Cataloging-in-Publishing Data

Names: Fittleworth, George.
Title: Deer poop or bear poop? / George Fittleworth.
Description: New York : Gareth Stevens Publishing, 2020. | Series: The scoop on poop | Includes glossary and index.
Identifiers: ISBN 9781538233399 (pbk.) | ISBN 9781538229545 (library bound) | ISBN 9781538233405 (6pack)
Subjects: LCSH: Deer–Juvenile literature. | Bears–Juvenile literature. | Animal droppings–Juvenile literature.
Classification: LCC QL737.U55 F58 2020 | DDC 599.65–dc23

Published in 2020 by
Gareth Stevens Publishing
111 East 14th Street, Suite 349
New York, NY 10003

Designer: Sarah Liddell
Editor: Therese Shea

Photo credits: Cover, p. 1 Jody./Shutterstock.com; p. 5 Inga Nielsen/Shutterstock.com; p. 7 stockphotofan1/Shutterstock.com; p. 9 Tom Reichner/Shutterstock.com; p. 11 L. E. MORMILE/Shutterstock.com; p. 13 Bruce MacQueen/Shutterstock.com; p. 15 critterbiz/ Shutterstock.com; p. 17 J. Bicking/Shutterstock.com; p. 19 (main) Mark Caunt/Shutterstock.com; p. 19 (inset) K Steve Cope/Shutterstock.com.

Printed in the United States of America

CPSIA compliance information: Batch #CS19GS: For further information contact Gareth Stevens, New York, New York at 1-800-542-2595.

CONTENTS

Boldface words appear in the glossary.

On the Trail

You and your family are on a hike in the woods. The wind is brushing leaves together. You can hear other sounds, too. Animals are on the move. Suddenly, you look down and see a pile of poop near the path!

Deer or Bear?

You guess that the poop must come from a large animal because there's a lot of it! The largest animals in this forest are deer and bears. **Researching** these animals will help you find out which animal left this scat, or poop.

White-Tailed Deer

There are many deer **species**. White-tailed deer live all over North and South America. They're often seen in the woods. Males can be more than 6 feet (1.8 m) tall from hoof to head. They can weigh 400 pounds (181 kg), too!

White-tailed deer are **herbivores**. They eat whatever plants they can find, such as grasses, leaves, nuts, fruits, and branches. They also eat **lichens** and **fungi**. Deer usually eat at night or when there's less light, so they can be hard to spot!

Deer Scat

White-tailed deer have a four-part stomach that helps them **digest** plants. Sometimes they eat food, cough it up, and eat it again. Deer scat looks like dark oval **pellets**. It may be found in a pile. Deer poop more than 10 times a day!

Black Bears

Black bears are the most common bear species in North American forests. Some black bears are actually a brown color. Some have white markings, too. Black bears are large. Males can be 6 feet (1.8 m) long and weigh 600 pounds (272 kg)!

Black bears are omnivores. That means they eat meat and plants—whatever they can find! In some areas, they hunt young deer in the spring. Sometimes black bears eat trash people leave behind when they're camping. They eat dead animals, too. Yuck!

Bear Scat

Black bear scat often looks like tube-shaped clumps. It can be different colors depending on what the bear has been eating. If the bear has been eating mostly plants, its poop doesn't smell much. Bear scat can weigh 1 pound (0.5 kg)!

Whose Scat Is That?

So, which animal left the scat by the path? The poop you saw was dark brown and made up of little oval pellets. It wasn't a tube-shaped clump. It was a deer's scat! Knowing how to **identify** scat is a skill!

STUDY THE SCAT

	WHITE-TAILED DEER	BLACK BEAR
WHERE DOES IT LIVE?	NORTH AND SOUTH AMERICA; IN THE WOODS	NORTH AMERICA; IN THE WOODS
WHAT SHAPE IS ITS SCAT?	OVAL PELLETS; MAY BE IN A PILE	OFTEN TUBE-SHAPED CLUMPS
WHAT COLOR IS ITS SCAT?	DARK BROWN OR BLACK	USUALLY DARK, BUT CHANGES COLOR WITH FOOD

IT WAS THE DEER'S POOP!

GLOSSARY

digest: to break down food inside the body so that the body can use it

fungus: a living thing that is somewhat like a plant, but doesn't make its own food, have leaves, or have a green color. Fungi include molds and mushrooms.

herbivore: an animal that eats only plants

identify: to find out the name or features of something

lichen: a small plantlike living thing that grows on rocks and walls

pellet: a small, hard ball of something

research: studying to find something new

species: a group of plants or animals that are all of the same kind

FOR MORE INFORMATION

BOOKS

Jeffries, Joyce. *Black Bears.* New York, NY: PowerKids Press, 2016.

Lawrence, Ellen. *Poop Detectives.* New York, NY: Bearport Publishing, 2018.

Mara, Wil. *Deer.* New York, NY: Cavendish Square Publishing, 2014.

WEBSITES

American Black Bear
www.nationalgeographic.com/animals/mammals/a/american-black-bear/
Read more about black bears, also called American black bears.

Fun Deer Facts for Kids
www.sciencekids.co.nz/sciencefacts/animals/deer.html
There's a lot more to know about these four-legged creatures!

INDEX